WAS GENGHIS KHAN REALLY MEAN?

Biography of Famous People

Children's Biography Books

Genghis Khan was the Supreme Khan of the Mongols from 1206 until 1227. He was born in 1162 and died in 1227. He was most known for being the Founder of the Mongol Empire.

Read further to learn about his life and accomplishments, then you can decide if he really was a mean person.

Not much is known about his personal life or his appearance, even though he was a very influential person. There are no surviving portraits or sculptures, and what information is available is unreliable or contradictory. He is mostly described as strong and tall, and having a flowy mane of hair with a bushy, long beard.

One of the more surprising descriptions comes from the 14th century chronicler Rashid al-Din, claiming that Genghis had green eyes and red hair. This account, however, is questionable since he had never met him. However, these features were known to be possible among the Mongols who were an ethnically diverse tribe.

خواجه رشيدالدين فضل اله
مورخ و وزير دانشمند
Rashid-al-Din

Memorial of Genghis Khan

EARLY LIFE

Genghis was raised on the cold, harsh Mongolia plains. As a boy, he was known by the name Temujin, meaning "finest steel". Yesugai, his father, was the khan (chief) of the tribe. Temujin enjoyed his childhood, even though it was difficult. He liked to hunt with his brothers, and he also enjoyed riding horses.

Even as a child, he had to contend with the brutal life of the Mongolian Steppe. The rival Tatars had poisoned his father when he was nine, and he and his family then became expelled from their own tribe and his mother was left to raise her seven children by herself.

Mongolian Steppe

Genghis was raised foraging and hunting for survival, and as a child he may have killed his half-brother in a fight over food. As a teenager, he and his young wife were abducted by rival clans and he had to spend time in slavery prior to making an escape. In spite of these hardships, by his 20s he had demonstrated himself to be a formidable leader and warrior.

After gathering supporters, he forged alliances with heads of many important tribes. By 1206, he was already successful in consolidating the steppe confederations within his banner and then proceeded to move on to outside conquests.

MARRIED

At the young age of nine, he was sent off to live with Borte, his future wife, and her tribe. After a few years had passed, he found out that his father was poisoned by the enemy Tartars, and returned home to become Khan of his home tribe.

BETRAYED

When Temujin returned home, he found that another warrior had betrayed his family, taking over the role of khan, and then proceeded to kick Temujin and his family out of the tribe. They were barely able to survive on their own, but he was not ready to give up. He and his family were able to survive the horrendous winter and he then began plotting revenge against the Tartars.

BUILDING AN ARMY

Temujin began building his own tribe during the next few years. He proceeded to marry Borte and became aligned with her tribe. He was known to be a brutal and fierce fighter, admired by the Mongols because of his courage. He continued to build his army of warriors until it was large enough, and forceful enough, to overtake the Tartars.

REVENGE ON THE TARTARS

Once he had fought the Tartars, he showed no remorse. He went on to decimate their army and killed their leaders. He began conquering the enemy Mongol tribes. He knew they needed unity. Once he had conquered his greatest enemy, the other Mongol tribes followed him. They called him Genghis Khan, meaning "ruler of all".

A BRILLIANT GENERAL

Genghis became a brilliant general. He called his soldiers "gurans" and organized them in groups of about 1000. They would train every day on battle tactics and would use smoke signals, drums, and flags for sending messages throughout his army quickly. They were well-armed and trained to ride horses and fight starting at a very young age.

They controlled their horses by only using their legs and would fire deadly arrows as they rode at full speed. He was also known to use innovative strategies on the battlefield. He would on occasion send in small forces and then have them retreat. Once their enemy charged back at the smaller force, they would find themselves surrounded by a pack of the Mongol warriors.

Jebe became one of his best generals. He had once been an enemy that shot Genghis during battle using an arrow. Genghis was impressed and spared Jefe's life. Jebe became known as "The Arrow".

LEADER

Genghis Khan was known to be a strong leader. He may have been cruel and lethal to the enemies, but he was loyal to those who believed in him. He launched a written code of law which came to be known as the Yasak. He would promote soldiers who performed well, regardless of their background. He expected his own sons to perform well if they desired to be leaders.

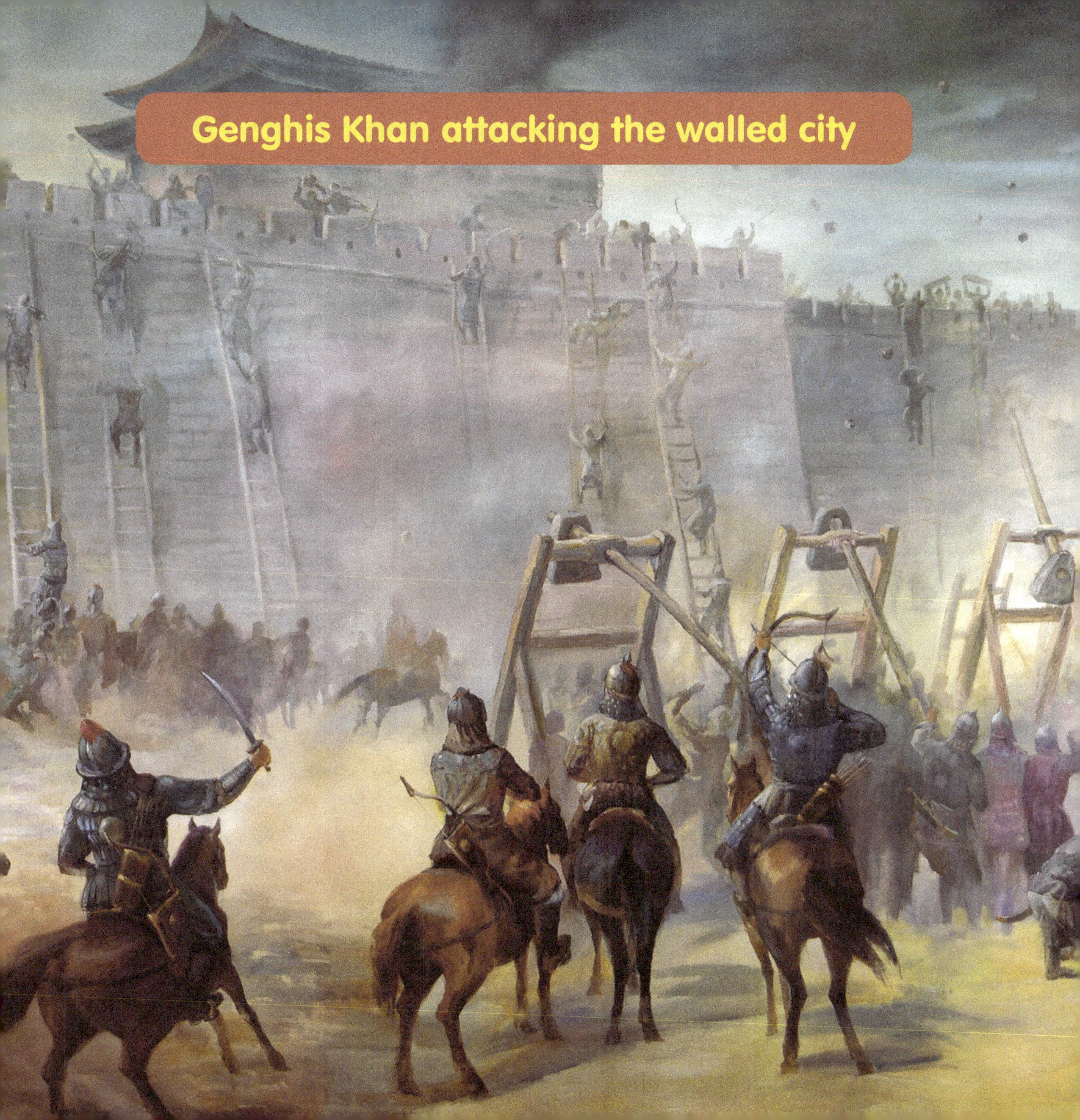

Genghis Khan attacking the walled city

Genghis Khan monument

CONQUESTS

Once the Mongol tribes were united, he turned to the south. In 1207, he attacked the Xi Xia people. It took him only two years to defeat the Xi Xia and they surrendered. He turned to China's Jin Dynasty in 1211. He wanted revenge for the way they treated the Mongols. He captured Yanjing (Beijing), Jin's capital city by 1215, and the Mongols now ruled the northern area of China.

Even though it is difficult to know definitively how many people died throughout the Mongol conquests, it is reported by historians that the number is approximately 40 million. The censuses obtained from the Middle Ages indicate that China's population plunged by tens of millions during his lifetime and some scholars believe that he killed three-fourths of Iran's modern day population during the time he was at war with the Khwarezmid Empire. All together, these attacks might have reduced the population of the world by 11 percent.

Statue of Genghis Khan at Marble Arch

Genghis Khan mausoleum

MUSLIM LANDS

He desired establishment of trade with Muslim lands towards the west. A trade delegation was sent to for a meeting with its leaders. One city's governor, however, had the men killed. Genghis became furious.

He proceeded to take up command of 200,000 warriors and the next several years were spent destroying the western cities. He proceeded as far as Eastern Europe, destroying anything and everything. He became merciless, and left no one to live.

The Kwarizmian Empire was the name of the land towards the west. Its leader was Shah Ala ad-Din Muhammad. In 1221, this dynasty ended as he had both the Shah and his son killed.

DEATH

He died in 1227, after returning to China. Many believe that he injured himself as he fell from a horse, but no one knows for sure how he died. Other sources report anything from a wound to the knee by an arrow as well as malaria. Another more questionable account reports that he was murdered as he tried to rape a Chinese princess.

CHINGGIS KHAAN

Once he died, however, we went to great lengths to keep secret his final place of rest. Legend indicates that during his funeral procession, everyone was slaughtered that they came into contact with so they would not be able to tell where he was to be buried.

Horses were then repeatedly ridden over the grave in order to conceal it. More than likely, his tomb is around or on Burkhan Khaldun, a Mongolian mountain, but the precise location remains a mystery.

Burkhan Khaldun

Genghis Khan is now known to be a national hero and Mongolia's founding father. However, during the Soviet rule of the 20th century, merely mentioning his name had been banned.

Hopeful that they could erase all evidence of Mongolian nationalism, they tried suppressing his memory by forbidding people to make pilgrimage to Khentii, his birthplace, as well as deleting his story from textbooks.

CHINGGIS KHAAN
INTERNATIONAL AIRPORT
ОЛОН УЛСЫН ИРЭХ НИСЛЭГ
INTERNATIONAL ARRIVALS
ОРОН НУТГИЙН ИРЭХ НИСЛЭГ
DOMESTIC ARRIVALS

Eventually, his name was restored to Mongolian history after winning independence early in the 1990s. He has since become recurring in popular culture and art. His portrait now appears on its currency and the nation's airport in Ulan Bator is named for him.

His legacy is significant. His successors, including Kublai Khan who was his grandson, completed conquest of China and maintained control over it from many years. Ogedei, Genghis' immediate successor, ruled the Mongol Empire during its greatest extent, from Korea in the east to Poland in the west, approximately 11 million square miles, comparable to the size of Africa. One benefit of this seizure was consolidation of rule over Silk Road, streamlining communication and trade between West and East.

Kublai Khan

Genghis was known to be an intolerant and brutal man, creating death and destruction. The people he conquered felt negatively towards him because of his brutality.

As you have learned, Genghis Khan was a very powerful leader, but was he mean? Think about it and decide for yourself. For additional information go to your local library, research the internet, and ask questions of your teachers, family, and friends.

Visit
BABY PROFESSOR
EDUCATION KIDS
www.BabyProfessorBooks.com
to download Free Baby Professor eBooks
and view our catalog of new and exciting
Children's Books